MYSTERIUM

Marion Fawlk

First published jointly in the UK by PhotoStroud
and Chrysalis Poetry
5 Oxford Terrace, Uplands
Stroud, Glos GL5 1TW

Poems previously published:

'Commitment' and 'Aloneness'
were first published in *Into the Further Reaches*
Editor Jay Ramsay, PS Avalon, 2007

'Wild Dancer', 'Music for Wild Horses', 'Union' and 'Blue Spirit'
were first published in *Earth Ascending*
Editor Jay Ramsay, Stride, 1997

'Delighting in Rainbows' was first
performed at St Martin-in-the-Fields, London
in collaboration with composer Rosemary Duxbury

ISBN: 978-1-906662-06-6

Dedication

For Richard and Simon

Acknowledgements

To Jay Ramsay whose selfless dedication to the art of poetry has the capacity to transfrom lives. With endless gratitude for showing me how soul can live upon the earth.

And for those who have given me heart for the journey: Nicholas Bechgaard, Gabriel Bradford-Millar, Naomi Brandel, Carole Bruce, Cheryl and Donald Cordery, Sam Cordery, Rosemary and Mike Duxbury, Sybil Edwards, Prue Fitzgerald, Maria Fischer, Rod and Alice Friend, Lucy Lidell, Rob and Jehanne Mehta, Genie Poretzki-Lee, Yvan Roux, Sharon St Clair, Fatieh Saudi, Peter D Scott, Rachel Stevens, Bob Swan, Emma Tame, Sam Urquhart, Hannah Whyman, Michael Williams, Gilly Wyatt-Smith and Simon Zussman.

Stroud Community: Jo, Neil and Moina, Stroud Valleys Artspace, Fred Chance, Kel Portman and PhotoStroud.

Fez Community: Alla and Kate, David Amster, Cafe Clock, Cleo Brun, Omar Chennafi, Cecille, Camille and Fattah, Erich Groat, Helen, Josephine, Karima, Mokri Family, Rachida, Susannah and Sandy, Tessa and Anne, the Twins, Zara and Adam and Dr Ziani.

Preface

Not all poetry needs to sound like journalism in verse. Poetry which has a visionary and sacred emphasis draws on something timeless because of the dimension it describes. Marion Fawlk writes in the vatic tradition of oral chant, spell-making, prayers, as she says, 'incantations' where the feminine is respected, is temple and place of initiation which a woman in any time needs to find in order to enter into her own depth of being and becoming.

Her poems are portals into the imagination which takes place inside her female consciousness of self (gender) and spirit (true being). And her consciousness of what she is doing here in her craft, and the labour of its inception, creates a unique scriped utterance unlike anything (or anyone) else I know of that might also explain how an only child born in the Forest of Dean can also carry a knowledge distilled from centuries.

Rimbaud's prophecy in a letter of May 1871 (he was 17 at the time) comes to mind: and there will be poets like this! When the eternal slavery of Women is destroyed, when she lives for herself and through herself, when man – up till now abominable – will have set her free, she will be a poet as well! Woman will discover the unknown! Will her world of ideas differ from ours? She will discover strange things, unfathomable, repulsive, delightful; we will accept and understand them.

That acceptance and understanding still has to take place; and this collection, with its awareness of the deeper virginal state of the woman who is at one in herself, its insight into the deeper nature of love that can only be based on freedom, and the deeper cycles of death and rebirth, is profoundly a part of it.

Jam Ramsay
Stroud, 2009

I believe there is something of the divine mystery in everything that exists. We can see it sparkle in a sunflower or a poppy. We sense more of the unfathomable mystery in a butterfly that flutters from a twig – or in a goldfish swimming in a bowl. But we are closest to God in our own soul. Only there can we become one with the great mystery of life. In truth at very rare moments we can experience that we ourselves are that divine mystery.

Plotinus

I remember the day wonder came, rose up under my skin like some exotic guest. It appeared uninvited singing its own song. I was four years old, peonies bloomed and I was lost in them. I visited daily drawn by their foreignness. This was something newly found, a visual response to beauty which changed the atmosphere inside my bones. I only knew that my heart had found an opening, spreading as if deep in the earth of an unseen world. I was that earth and host to its seeds. It was my first encounter with paradox, that the seen and the unseen are one. The beauty, the mystery inherent in the peony was also inherent in me. It gave to me the dreaming eye, and I was entered evermore into the dreaming realm of the psyche.

In order to speak anew we must first journey beyond utterance, trusting the alchemy of silence, the fluency of its inner script and the gifts of its evocations. It is the poet's way, the way of vision and the unassailable power of divination and magic.

Marion Fawlk

Contents

MUSE

Invisible one
Surviving voice of numinous currents
Swift are your callings
Doves of manna
Tracking breath
Between armour and sealed veins

Trajectories known to petrels
Mockingbirds
And sea borne winds

You are the godstar
That clings to this hair of fire
These syllables of dew

You beat an aorta of feathers
In a hollow of frenzied blood
Unlettered tapers
Virginal alphabets
Burning plumed magic
Into my coolness

SABBATHS OF EVE

l am the wild apple's daughter
Pulp of the old mythology
A dialect of lightening
Coupled with God
In the thicket of my own plenitude

The deeper hymen
Was never taken
Epiphanies
Like swallowed moons
Flash in ardent groves

When I sing
ln the Sabbaths of Eve
Libations
Buried in bones
Wash around the waist of her temple

MOONTIDE

I must go to the dark hut
In this my time of brooding
Moontide flow
When femaleness imprints
Her marking speck

Questing without searching
My waters fall
With furious intent
I cannot pull against this tide
And must allow these gifts
Spread before the table
Of my Lord

Wisdoms
They are not mine
But journey like the moon
Through chosen nights
And l am vested
With some moonlit star
To shine bright

And so
These words are broken
Through my blood
The sacrament is body of this flesh
I taste your words here
And upon the table of the dark hut
I will bless your name
With berries of red wine

THE SOURCE

Shadow my face
For it is not here that I live

My secrets are poised innermost

My mouth shines in the cave

And my breasts hang like a glorious ladder

I move in the sudden depths
Soundless
Not of ether

But here in airless chambers

I spread myself unconcerned
Plunged beyond the neck of the world

Where my grit is choice

And my tongue is glazed with bedrock

I have entered
Through a bloodless cord

She sings my name

The Queen of the dark womb

She seeds me fair bellied

And all utterance is hers

I am the progeny of rising
I am the progeny of descent
Such is her wisdom

She embraces me in wilderness

And in the winter ice of tundra

Intuitive the vessel
That bears my earthing bone

Her hands have shaped me long
In the halls of mine inheritance

I rise
A voice of flowering

Her sword tip bound with rose

GODDESS

Hail Kore
Hail Persephone
The earth is velvet touch
Eyes have met thee there
Shadowed
In the flanks of dark split night
Mould of deepest yew
Thy membrane keeping
Pummel the cairn
Uplift the stone
For turn we will
In the four quartered loom
Spin the weald
Spin the circuitous route of stars
Hair of receding crone
Hair of all coiling virgin
Speak to us as Mother
All creatures know thy silver
And thy trackless ways
Concealer
Benevolent stem of rooting birth
Plunge us
Hollow us
As a sounding bell within the circle
Dancer of flames
Ignite the flesh
Of the sentient sleepers
And bring us forth
With newborn cries
From thy living womb of truth

DAUGHTER OF EARTH

Seeking herbage
She gathers totems for her soul

Sniffs the air

Consumes silence

Imagining vixens
She spins her quest
With the sleekness of fur
Fingers her mind with feral juices

She is wild and black-eyed

An Empress

Requiring mountains

Her throne is a solemn place of rock
She sits with the stillness of hawks
The slow burn of passion
Imbibing magic

She is mutant
Steeped in the laws of universe
Becoming owl
The green lake of marshes

Her woman's voice is loud
A javelin of fulminous belief
Drawn from the bloodshine of knowing

She takes thunder to her heart

Calls up the gods from her deep bellied drum

Smears herself with lineage

She is the imprint of cycles
A sorceress of ashes
The daughter returned

She is the fruit
The barefoot skin of forgotten tribes
Fired in the dance of earth

SISTER OF EARTH

You lie
Shaft rim of syllable

Etched into grass

Birdfoot touch on a green vein
Where you

Are
The blade spear

Flesh undone
Streamed into ochre

Flanks abandoned
Into

The pallet earth

Of dreams

Where scent
Is
A mirror light
Untarnished

And we

Are no more
Than one single moment
Of perfect reflection

Your body is spread

Like a valley

And l see you
Dipped in a funnel of harebell
Fragile
Like yourself

Sea glass transmitter
Diadem of light thrust
That can shatter
Or illuminate
You Bend
On a tune of lacewing
Through
Open throats of flowers

Diffusing paradise

And you
In your heart's streaming

Infuse

The wonder of first love
Breath spindled
Without knowing
Taking

Petals
Into your vast capacity
Centre of gold

Where healing and beauty
So delicately lie

I see you there

You

On the green grass

Behind your shadow
Pears hang
Testament of blossom
Witness of Spring

I tread
Not wanting to disturb

Bearing the earth's gift
For your table

And you

Turn

Flushed by the sun

Still
With the flower

Soft on your face

WILD DANCER

Shoulder the wind
Trail the valley wild with wood speech

Taste the underlit spells
The unity of grasses bound in hips of sky

You are the flame

The green spark

Finding always the unspoken rhythms

The verdant watcher

Bared to prophesy

It is in your running body
Your snake-eyed dancer
That all truths unite
Converge in ecstasy

Bliss
Unwinding the forward nature
The outreaching harmonies

There is no canker
No aborted fruits
Only the golden spears
The grain
Calling to the honeybee

Your body

The flower

The vessel

The rich liana

The primitive ground

Fondle the incantations

The drum of the lover

The liquid moon

Risen is the power
The worldless vortex
Shimmered
In your immortal branches

Taking all you have conceived
Into
The voluptuous curves of paradise

COMMITMENT

Commitment
Comes of itself
It evolves
It is not made

It is not a treatise of martyrdom
Or an act of bargaining exchange

Its power

Lies in the naked truth of feelings

Its refinement
Is lack of possession

It is a free land

And grows from its own liberated centre

UNION

I love you

In the soul of the one body

All passions spilt

To a point beyond distinctions

Transmuting sex

Into the nameless

Man of Woman

Woman of Man

I honour you

And set your free

Where androgyny has no fences

DESIRE

You, speak with tongueless hands
Prowling, eloquently

Through the shanks of my tethered bones

Artfully, puncturing
The lid of sighs
Eating them as they spew

Into your deep palmed forays

My blood is a river of quickened lights
Buzzing with each dynamic syllable

Alert

Tuned

To a universe of vulvic flood
Her dedicated presence

Hungry for Sabbaths and the Horned God

Your words
Oil the camp of my loins

Secretions
From the agents of darkness

Pour with the weight of silence

Moist notes
Holding the unbetrayed sounds

The call of the father seed
Ovum mouthed

Roaring like beasts between us

GRIEF

Effigies
Cry like wounds

Weary children from burning cities
Join my lamentations
Keen for that which is lost

The home of love
Destroyed
Become no more than a begging bowl
Empty

Am I this ragged creature
Reflected
In a face of ashes
Your dull flame
Grey upon my soul

The mask you give me
Stifles breath
Life
Holds no future
Dishonours the chalice given

Hostile tongues
Bequeath a jagged silence
Taking even God
Into the mourning chamber

Grief is a dead cell
Burning its name on the altar
This is also love

Tears
Moistening the stone
As the seed falls between ruins

DARK MOTHER

Dark mother

You lie a furtive reaper

Staged where woman's lore

Has no kirtle or hiding place

The formidable edicts of your sceptered ways

Carry the untranslatable questions

Into the oracles of change

You bring me as a wraith

Before my considered time of dying

Demanding my death

Whilst I danced for you in connubial lights

My earth is a torn scabbard

Bereft of sword

Assigning the vertical

To your implacable senses

There is no rising mage

Only the revelations of surrender

As I cast all known prophesies

Onto the refining blades

Of a greater harvest

DARK LIGHT

My dark woman
Holds fierce cries

A thousand losses
Buried in white chalk smiles

I swing in a soul of unflinching belief
Take my mending
Into the arms of Gaia
Give to her my raw terrors
My fear of life's scaffolds

I am afraid
Only in her can I undress
The ingratitude of wounds

Announce to her green conjouring
Her breath of witchery
The willingness
To be cut again into the quick of life

She promises a flute
From my sack of thorns

Am I ready to enter spring
From my breast of bruised colours

Sorrow expires in dead leaves

Gaia
Seed your exultant shoots

Into this thinning heart

AMBER

I am empty

Split to a place without the beloved

Sectioned where muscles of love
Ache for walls of intimacy

This patch of unshared self

Says

Give me the edge of another

Holding amber

Like an angel

To sweeten the dark

MIRAGE

There is no green sward

No purple tips

Burnished odiferous

By the sweet inhalation of sun

I am a mirage

Un-breathed

Spat out

Betwixt night and the space of dawn

In the pinch of a black net

Boneless

I long to weave an artless globe

Feel earth and sky

The procreating trunk of oak

Ardent

Spreading life

Into fernless country

ALONENESS

Aloneness
Is a time of contemplation
The renewal of vows
Of containment in the sacred heart
It is not didactic
Or of intellectual persuasions
It is the living prayer of relationship
Of being with what is

Aloneness
Is not the anger of the wound
Or the warrior fires of Kali
It is the time of robing
And of the veil

It is the beauty of the bride
The ritual of marriage

It is the reverie
Of the holy spirit
The consummation of the blest

POETRY IS

A perception of self
Beyond parameters
It is indelible ink
On a fleshy page

And the incipient route of excess

It is the echo of God
At vanishing point
And the sacred place
Of temples

It is the dancer
Finely balanced
On a pale edged beam
Tuned to a whisper

Poetry is the consciousness of light

It is the unified flash
Of articulate vibrato
That strikes
A waiting silhouette

It is the word
The luminaire of birth
And the gold leaf
Shine of subtleties

Poetry is space in the elemental womb

It is the primal
Voice released
And found
In the answering
Call of windchimes

SOUL BIRD

This bird has feathered strange bones

Certainly knows the blue light of ravens

Is skeletal

Tears hauntings out of rock

Avoids capture

Denies plummeting

Consults no trembled hours

Is as thin as the wind

A piping of air

A note of distance

Is the kiss of God

On the mark of time

LOURDAS LEAF

You

Born into leaf time

Dance your molecular body

Into mine

Everything is alive

Manifesting form

Manifesting the unmanifested

You

Born into leaf time

The stillness of your beauty

Is All

Is All

ESSENCES

We are the dust of pollen
So let our breath be

Golden
Shower of the invisible impulse

We are the iridescent wing
So let our loving be

Gracious
Unfolding from notes unspoken

We are the temperament of air
So let our spirit be

Fragrant
Scent of the rose immortal

We are the immensity of sky
So let our hearts be

Holding
Sunset and sunrise of man

We are the clay of earth
So let our souls be

Malleable
Shaped to the will divine

THE HEALING

How can we honour pain
Recognise the celebrant
In the shards of dissolution

This is the mystery
Taking us deeper than we know

Enshrined
Upheld in the soul's quintessence
The kernel of light in our darkness
Healing the wounds

Even as we

Weep

BREATH OF LIGHT

Praise Be

The final spiracle of life

Entrance and exit of the incandescent cell

The breathing pore of angels

Through all the vital years

Febrile magics burn

Regathering secrets of the soul's ingress

Delivering

Unsealed at the earth spent hour

The immaculate song

Hymn of the body

Breath of light

A footprint of stars

In the humming gold

COLOURS OF DARKNESS

In the dark wheel
A world is turning
Poppies bloom
Red veined

On feathers of black wings
An orange bow
Lies firm in your hand

And a blue flame
Invites the knave

To trim a lamp with gold

Ice flows melt
And silent sisters
Wait on banks of green

The iris
Blues your path with vision
And white gods
Raise a circled
Land

Sequenced
Beyond
Imagining

INITIATE

You step naked
Into the silence of humility
No artifice of words
To mask your adoration

You are air

Imbued with the spirit of colours
That only the soul can shape

Into your breath
Is born
Another
Wider

Expanding vision
Shared by ancients

And you
In this green time
Of new beginnings
Feel the same sap rise

In a body

Outstretched

Like a canticle
Given to the earth
Where the heartbeat
Of your nakedness
Is the father
Of all emerging beauty

GATEWAYS

Confirm, confirm
Let this be the pilgrimage
Unlock the gateways of the heart
Forestalling not with dross imaginings

The flames of the high altar
Burn continually
Make your footsteps swift
Linger not on the low plains
But lift yourself
On frequencies of the higher heavens

Arch your soul

Your spirit is strong
It carries the cord of your birthright
Let this be the bridge
Bestowed in the cradle of stars

The map lies in the palm
Your flesh the patterned compass
Of transition
Allow the points
Falter not in their direction
Your voyage is foresworn
Naked in the cell of truth

Stand in the memories
That pulse the blood
And cross the borderline
Speaking in tongues of holy
Affirmation

DELIGHTING IN RAINBOWS

I sleep
In clouds of morning
Where the fist of dark waters
Holds

My slumbering
Immortality

Known
To the eye of the palm
Waiting
For light
And the open hand of rainfall

I lie
Soft as a dawn seed
Born
Into the stillness
Of this
Opulent pool

Filling me
Diffusing me
Until the moment

Shines
In a raindrop

The Voice
That has shaped me
Wakens me with light
And l am glad
To be small

A particle
Of this
Where my face
Is
Joy
Coloured with infinitude

I am
changed

Become
miracle

And
In the company of rainbows
Find
My final transformation

LAKES OF GOLD

The moon sings in the high places
And she the child
Walks steadfast on the shore

She moves
No ordinary dancer
But with some rhythmical incline

Pulsed beyond the shadowing of limbs

She nets the veiling light
And murmurs where the dreaming orb
Is low

She is the wing
Preparing for the flight
The gentle arc
That curves the fluted call

Her innocence
Distillates regard
Drifting
Through the portals of exchange

She is the line
The whitening arrow of the rose
She is companion of invisibles

And treads the final measure

Where the lakes are trimmed with gold

THE GOLDEN FACE

For the joy of you
I cast this seal
Like a costly jewel
From the love of the heart

Perfectly shaped
I place it
Unspoken
On thy brow

Bright one
You come from the seeding wing
Of angels
Always the halfmoon pearl
Shaded
In the sacred breath of me

Now when veils of time
Are shed
And only at the appointed hour
You render yourself
As a golden mark
Of exaltation

Standing vertical
In your flame
Of light

I did not question
Your emergence
But sent a winged portion
Of my love
Into the glassen rib
We share

O Bright one
United from long forgotten shores
The mysteries newly sung
I hear your holy self
And you are shining
I embrace you
In a secret pool
Of calm

And gather you
In the dream
That is forever swiftly
Flowing

MUSIC FOR WILD HORSES

Wild horses came to the gate
That stood on the crest of night

Imperative the sound
That sped the dark wind

Limbs carried airborne
Consummate in needs that struck sinews
Blind to rider's clay

The magic of the ways
Known only to the wild beasts

In legacies of muted mothers blood

That sheds all confines

With kind and infinite alchemies

Fleet footed
Loosed of bridles
To join with beaded loins
In feast of darkness

All manacles of savage men
Torn
From stables where dry hay
Is not for your feeding mouths

The damp moss and loam of earth
And scent of growing corn

Brings you here
Instinct held

With hooves bright on scudding air

To high pastures
Where grasses
Grow abundantly in grace
And the dew is the sweetness
Of all your journeyings

ON WINGS OF LIGHT

In these latter days

They shall come as wings upon the air

Consciousness

Robed in streams of shriven light

Spiraling

From the stellar centres

This is the new allegiance

Kindled

In the sacred heart of man

The numberless fires of inner constellations

Manifesting spirit

To redeem the world

BLUE SPIRIT

You glitter, dark one

You contemplate this body of believers

You draw a gold coin

Tilting pale riders on coracles of air

You dance the white dream

Lipped to the earthwind

Where the rim crosses silence

There is no language

Only the emptying and the blue spirit

Tracing the wings of luminous choirs

To meet you, as we rise

CIRCLING

We met in the radiant body

As light we were

Circling

The presence between us

Closening

Separate

One

Innocent we were

Simple

A smile upon roundabouts

Children

All age dissolved

Emptied of names

Bliss filled

Existing

In diaphanous silence

Beautifully

LEAVES AND MOONS

The pen

Is a quiver of spells

Sweeping the firmament

For high magic

Touching

The numinous entities of stars

Unrolling the mystical

As leaves and moons

Fall

The mind turns

And seeks oblivion

BRIDGE OF SILENCE

To embrace the pause

Is to take the courage of silence

And let it fall

Believing in the continuous

The eternal beginnings

Silence has its own impulse

Sensual and slow

The glissando of change

In the bardo lands

Uncovering the new

From aborted husks of reality

RUDE PRAYERS

They come in side by side
A jostling of prayers

Like badly timed magicians

They have no sense of place

Each one insistent
Angular
Oblivious to crowds

I tell them
Do not stuff my throat
With all your songs

Syphon them off

Learn good manners

Try making a graceful entrance

They tell me

Etiquette stifles
Fills us with lead

Our sparks must fly

We are unapologetic

Catch us if you can

A GATHERING OF ANGELS

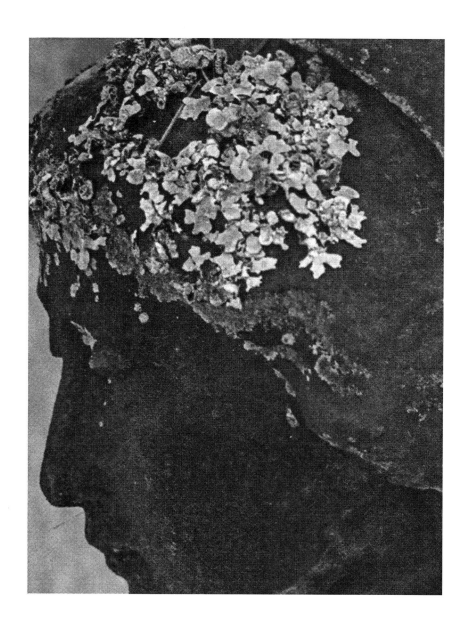

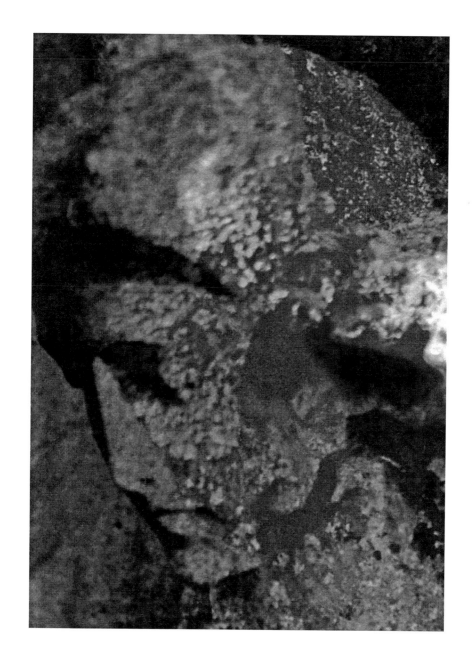

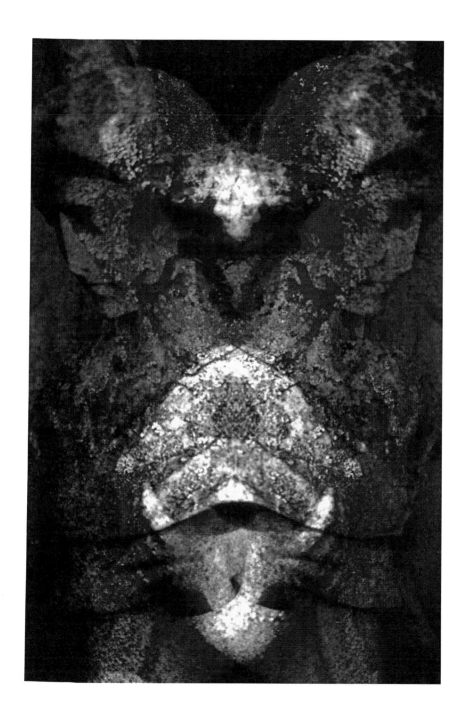